A WORLD OF DIFFE

A WORLD OF DIFFERENCE

by NORMAN MacCAIG

CHATTO & WINDUS

THE HOGARTH PRESS

LONDON

Published in 1983 by
Chatto & Windus · The Hogarth Press
40 William IV Street
London WC2N 4DF

The publisher gratefully acknowledges subsidy from the
Scottish Arts Council towards the publication of this volume.

British Library Cataloguing
in Publication Data

MacCaig, Norman,
    A world of difference.
    I. Title
    821'.914   PR6063.A/

    ISBN 0-7011-2693-0

Printed in Great Britain by
Redwood Burn Ltd
Trowbridge, Wiltshire

Contents

Helpless collector

Events come
bringing me presents —
more, as has been said, than the sands of the sea,
more, as has been said oftener, than the stars in the sky.

There's no refusal.

I'm the exultant possessor
of the ones that please me. I try to be
only the caretaker
of the ones I hate.

They won't let me.

I put the crooked mask
behind the delicate jar
and it moves to the front.

Legends

The kingfisher flies out to sea
and breeds in a special doldrum
created for it by the god of the winds.

The phoenix dies in her blazing nest
and, fluffing the ashes aside, rises again, all feathers,
in the suddenly glittering air.

That's what they thought
in the good old days.

Now it's men who do it. They go out
into the storms and wildernesses of thought
and create a ring of peace: where they breed
their own ferocious likenesses.

And others, crouched in a public place,
put fire to themselves. They burn,
and from their ashes rise
a miasma of horror, a stink of pity,
a semblance of the whole world.

Will the day come when they too
will be only legends that men will tell
to each other, saying
That's what they thought.
In those terrible times
that's what they thought.

Outsider

No battle in the thrush — grenade of song
in the tangled gean-tree.

No politics in the newt — fat-legged saurian
in its lascivious jungle.

Morality? The gannet angles down its Concorde head
and crash dives into the mackerel host.

A free world, a world without hypocrisy, without masks.

Cramped with humanity, I envy them.

And I watch the concept *freedom*, that quick-change artist,
put on still another disguise:
and I think, without comfort —
the gentle worm is sinuous as a lawyer
but pleads no special cases.

Two skulls

MacDiarmid found a pigeon's skull
on the bright shore turf of a Hebridean island.

I found the skull of a dogfish
on the sand at Cleethorpes.

His: the skull of a twirler and staller,
a rocketer, a headlong grace, symbol of peace.

Mine: a hooverer of the sea's floor, sneak thief
of herrings from nets, corpse-eater, emblem of nightmare.

After death the one is as beautiful as the other
(but not to a pigeon, not to a dogfish).

I hate death, the skull-maker, because he proves
that destroying and making happen together.

He'll be no friend of mine, as long as I'm still
a feathery pigeon or a scrapeskin dogfish.

— I mean a man, whose skull contains
ideas death never thought of.

They'll cheat him, for they'll lodge in another skull
— or become nothing, that comfortable absolute.

Invasion of bees

Between the ceiling and the roof
whole fields were humming.

Or, add to one bee a thousand others and it becomes
a dynamo.

A man was fetched from Helmsdale.
He carried a vicious brass pump.

It switched off that dynamo, it reaped
whole fields and heather slopes.

And a summer inside a summer
died, leaving a useless crop.

I have a summer inside my summer.
I cherish it. It's flowery and heathery.

Terrified, I dream of a man from Helmsdale
walking towards me, a sack in his hand.

From my window

Outside, there are gardens full of trees
that have not yet fruited and a silence
waiting to grow apples of music
and clustering berries of words.

If I could sweep away those clouds
a moon would stare at me,
uncomprehending, meaningless and lonely.

A truck goes by. In the noise it makes
there's a mutilated shape
struggling to become
a cousin of Beethoven, a sweet child
of Mozart.

A group of teenagers turns the corner.
Raucous voices. Dyed hair.
Tribal badges.

I stare down at them, like the moon,
uncomprehending, meaningless and lonely.

What visions are waiting to be born
in their sad eyes?
What loving gesture weeps for itself
in the angles of their arms?

Godot

I feel miserable, acting
their uncomprehending parts.
Don't they know they're waiting
for who's already there?

There I am, in their minds,
in their boots,
in the footlights: and worse,
in their incomprehension.

I can't even go
and sit in the audience,
since I'm there too.

I'm trapped. It seems
there's nothing to do
but wait
for something to happen.

Ceremonial

Under the arc lamps
the gorgeous knight
would strut if he could, if his robes
would let him.

In the half dark tens of thousands of faces
cheer, like tens of thousands of plates cheering
on a fifteen-acre table.

Is this to ridicule them? Is this
to ridicule the gorgeous, the most gorgeous knight?

Is this to ridicule the small boy
who can see nothing
but who cheers and cheers anyway
into the back of the man in front of him?

For another Crusade, for the sacking
of the Newest Jerusalem
with its rancid slums
and its cheering multitudes.

Pibroch: The Harp Tree

Pibroch, I make you a man
who could shake hands with Bach
and talk with him over a glass
of Spanish wine.

You would walk in, with your sack
of images that are brightly dark and darkly bright,
and Bach, emerging from a labyrinthine fugue,
would greet you with warmth and pleasure. He'd pour
the Spanish wine.

There'd be grave wings beating
in that room and happy silences
laughing to each other.

When you left, you'd return
to your crystal land of bogs and coloured rocks,
and Bach
would stretch his elbows sideways
like wings and fold them again and go back into
the labyrinth where he's never lost,
seeking, like you, the minotaur
that will crouch beside him
with his heavy horns,
with his beautiful, golden eyes.

Two thieves

At the Place for Pulling up Boats
(one word in Gaelic) the tide is full.
It seeps over the grass, stealthy as a robber.
Which it is.

— For old Flora tells me
that fifty yards stretch of gravel, now under water,
was, in her granny's time, a smooth green sward
where the Duke of Sutherland
turned his coach and six.

What an image of richness, a tiny pageantry
in this small dying place
whose every house is now lived in
by the sad widow of a fine strong man.

There were fine strong men in the Duke's time.
He drove them to the shore, he drove them
to Canada. He gave no friendly thought to them
as he turned his coach and six
on the sweet green sward
by the Place for Pulling up Boats
where no boats are.

Where we are

In the middle, inaudibly
a yellow flower dies giving birth to a yellow flower.

And the ghost of water climbs high into the air
to make a drop of water and another.

In the fireplace light cries *Let me out!*
and the coals eat themselves to free their prisoner.

Night blackens itself and we say, *A star!*
(The star climbs into us, into our darkness.)

And death smiles ruefully, thinking
how little he is understood.

Clio

Socrates was never more right
than when the hemlock set about killing him
from the feet up: he was, himself,
what his irony had always been.

His judges, who had never understood irony,
went on drinking with their handsome boys
and pretty slave girls,
went on trying to corner the market
in wheat and olive oil.

The Muse of history, yawning with boredom,
judges the judges and finds them guilty.
Poor Clio. She has long since failed to be amused
by irony, truth, lies, murder
and suicide.

Sighing, she licks her finger
and wearily
turns over another page.

City fog

The flagpole's kinky all the way up
and above the black canal tall towers
shimmy slowly
in their filthy seven veils.

Moses never thought of this
when he chatted with the Lord
on that funny mountain.

The light from the fruitshop window
tries to cross the road and can't.
The apples and bananas and grapefruit
have a TV look.

None of this bothered Aaron
drunkenly prancing with his chums
round his pretty golden calf.
(It was only the size of a teapot.)

Everything's baffled. Even the Tollcross clock
looks glum, as if it knew
five past ten might as well be
ten past five.

Meanwhile Moses keeps coming down
that mountain and Aaron
kicks higher, shouts louder and slobbers
down his bristly Jewish chin.

And all this in Edinburgh, where I dance
in my foggy way
round a tiny golden calf, ignoring
the thunder up there and the manic old man
clutching broken stones to his skinny bosom.

Summer idyll

Under a ferocious snowfall
of gulls and fulmars
a corner of the bay is simmering
with herring fry.

Into them slice
Assyrian hosts
of mackerel.

Sweet day, so cool, so calm, so bright . . .

Three porpoises pronounce
three puffs and cavalry charge
into the Assyrians.

Clouds lisp across the sky in a trance of silence.

Farther out, a commando of killer whales
grin and leap.
They're setting their ambush
for the cavalry.

And in the gentle West
a ladylike sunset
swoons
on the chaise-longue
of the Hebrides.

Penelope

I thought they needed no Women's Lib.
in your day. And yet, there you are,
stuck with a lot of drunks
and your knitting and all that laundry:
unable even to slip out to the Mysteries.

Never mind. A dog is dying on a dunghill
and there's a boat in the bay.

He'll soon be home and you'll live happily
ever after, as long as you don't listen to him
muttering in his sleep
names you never heard of,
names like Calypso, names like Nausicaa.

Zeno, and his like

When Achilles, furious
for having let himself get mixed up
in such a ridiculous affair,
passed the tortoise with his first stride,
he left behind, also,
stupid philosophy, that's been muttering
And yet . . . nevertheless . . . all the same . . .
ever since.

From where I sit

In any mist
I do not feel at home —
in the mist of the First Cause,
the fog of numbers,
the Chanel miasma
of Ergo and Q.E.D.

By my fire
Perhaps and Maybe
smoke cigarettes and get drunk
sipping pints of impossibility.

They are me
talking to myself,
while outside stalk
the gross idiocies of metres and kilograms,
and a priestly face
glares through the window, bellowing
the exact temperature of hell
and the statistics of eternity.

Also

You try to help, and what happens?
You hurt also.

You hoist a sail on a boat
and one day, gusted sideways,
the boat is scattered in timbers
round a slavering rock.

You put violets in water, and what happens?
They lose all their scent.

And you give absence and loneliness and fear
when you give love — that full sail,
that sweet water.

Circe

The strange wanderers — I was so good to them.
I disencumbered them
of their heavy embellishments, of their burdensome lies
and restored them to their truths. Pig was pig,
wolf was wolf, snake was snake.

But the gods, those bad civilisers,
came between me and Odysseus,
who sailed off with his companions, corrupt
with history, and left me desolate
for the one I loved, for the false image
of the one I'll never know.

Portrait bust

That's forcing it, he thought,
and kneaded the clay back into
its shapeless shape.

Then he patted it, pulled it,
pared shavings off it.
His eyes ping-ponged
between it and his model.

No good . . . No good . . . It's not *him*.

And he pummelled the clay again
into its original shapelessness
and thought to himself
That's better. That's more like it

and started spoiling it again.

Camera man

Six rods are dapping for sea trout
on Loch Baddagyle. Their blowlines each make
a bosomy downwind curve. Six bushy flies
ballet dance on the sunstruck water.

— See that boulder? In its toupee of heather
there's a wild cat watching me. Two topazes with ears.
. . . I tilt up and pan along my trail of mountains
from Ben More Coigach all the way to Quinag.

An old ewe brings me down to the earth
she stamps her forefoot on. I look at her implacable
whisky and soda eyes. She knows all a sheep
needs to know: she's a black-stockinged bluestocking.

And a spinnaker line has straightened. The water
explodes and shoots a sea trout into the air,
while five bushy flies still dance on the moving glitter,
little water nymphs in their dangerous tutus.

Every day

What's that cart that nobody sees
grinding along the shore road?

Whose is the horse that pulls it, the white horse
that bares its yellow teeth to the wind?

They turn, unnoticed by anyone,
into the field of slanted stones.

My friends meet me. They lift me from the cart and,
the greetings over, we go smiling underground.

Enough

I don't want to shuffle in a Greek Theatre
chanting powerful platitudes
while Nemesis, off-stage, gouges and stabs.

Or twangle a harp in an Irish castle
while the drunken louts, the great heroes,
quarrel over chess or lie with a snake-brained woman.

I don't want to be one of those who paused
between the walls of the Red Sea and thought with longing
of Egypt and the simmering fleshpots.

Enough for me to watch a new ice age
grind down the high tops of Scotland, the harbours
without a boat, the frozen minds
without a song.

Daedalus

He made a mousetrap
and his PRO man
called it a labyrinth.

It was to catch a mouse —
the local papers
called it a minotaur.

In the film they made of it
Theseus and Ariadne
got bit parts.

But the spectators loved them
(projections of themselves)
and called them stars.

Then he made his mistake.
He forced his son
to follow in daddy's wing-beats.

Icarus rebelled and fell
through the generation gap
into mythology.

In his way he won — his name
is on the map,
which is more than his father's is.

Ugly waking

My early morning bird, sweet blackbird, starts
his early morning song. His note
never trembles.

And light begins to creep
along wires and shamelessly
to peer into windows.

I stir as though freed from ropes
and my morning thought begins
to speak in my head.

How its voice trembles.
How it flinches from the window
and won't look out.

I lie in a wretched darkness with no song in it
and with new ropes on me
made of light.

On a beach

There's something I want to forget,
though I forget what it is.

. . . My mind niggles and grits
like the sand under my feet.

I used to know things I didn't know.
Not any more. Now I don't know
even the things I know, though I think I do.

. . . Little waves slide up the beach and slide back,
lisping all the way. The moon
is their memory. In my head
there's no moon.

What I don't know I don't even think I know.
That was Socrates, conceited man.

I'm trying to remember
what I've remembered to forget.

Twenty yards away, a seal's head
looks at me
steadfastly
then tucks itself
under the surface, leaving
no ripple.

Running bull

All his weight's forward.
He looks like a big black hunchback
with a small black boy running behind him.

Put an invisible sixpence on the ground —
he'll turn on it.
So don't, if he's facing away from you.

People scatter. I scatter too.

Sometimes he stops
and looks redly around, wondering
which new direction
to hurtle at.

Donald saunters towards him.
The bull glowers at him
from between his knees.

And his fire goes out!. . .He puts on a nonchalance
and swaggers towards the byre, followed
by sauntering Orpheus.

A new age

Before the barbarians came —
Dante tried to describe it
in all those cantos. Hieronymus Bosch tried to paint it
but he, even he, fell short of the truth.
And Goya . . .

When the barbarians came, things were better.
They even let us wear our clothes
when we went into the gas chambers.
And what gratitude we felt
when they killed the mothers before
they killed their babies and when they blew off
the head of the Holy Prelate
without gouging his eyes out first.

How could we express our thankfulness
when the mass graves were filled
only with the dead?

We even revived the art of prayer. *O Lord*, we prayed,
we thank Thee for Thy present mercies,
we thank Thee for leading us forth
from the dark ages of civilisation.

Hermes–Mercury

Hermes was a bad god, a shifty fellow,
a liar, a thief, a teller of the future
(with dice, of course), a musician,
herald and messenger of the gods.

No wonder mercury was called after Mercury.
No wonder the Romans gave him that name:
the Trader, the Business Man.

How he must have laughed when the Romans
raised a statue to him
— god of commerce, god of profit and loss —
in the Street called Sober Street
where no shops were allowed, no pubs.

No wonder he was the conveyor of dreams.
Garden of Bliss, Vision of Hell — what did he care?
Yet I admire him. He was a survivor.

What a god, to survive among
those other gods and goddesses, those arrogant,
selfish, high-living turncoats and lechers —
too stupid to notice they were only
the blind dupes of Fate.

. . . Fate must have loved him, the black sheep,
the con man, the wide boy of Olympus.

Old couple in a bar

They sit without speaking, looking straight ahead.
They've said it all before, they've seen it all before.
They're content.

They sit without moving: Ozymandias and Sphinx.

He says something! — and she answers, smiling,
and taps him flirtatiously on the arm:
Daphnis and Chloe: with Edinburgh accents.

Below the Clisham, Isle of Harris: after many years

On the mountain pass to Maraig
I met an old woman
darker but only just
than the bad weather we were in.

She was leading a cow by a rope
all the way round the mountain
to Tarbert.

She spoke to me in a misty voice,
glad to rest, glad to exercise
her crippled, beautiful English.

Then they trudged on, tiny
in a murky space
between the cloud of the Clisham
and a tumbledown burn.

And I suddenly was back home again
as though she were her people's history
and I one of her descendants.

Family of long-tailed tits

Their twittering isn't avant-garde
or confessional or aleatory.
It doesn't quote other birds
or utter manifestos telling them
how to sing.

It's congruent with their way of flying,
for that, too,
is a sweetest, softest twittering
to the eye.

The clumsy, clever human
bumbles about in the space
between his actions and his words.
No congruence there.

He listens with envy
while their song flirts
from one twig of silence
to another one.

Gentle trap

I put my mind out there
like a bird table. On it I lay
a few crumbs of love, a grain or two
of admiration and one wriggling wish
asking to be noticed.

It works.

A thrush, two greenfinches
and a dunnock.

I'm pleased, but not satisfied.
What do you do to bring down
an eagle, a Great Auk,
a lammergeier?

Once a flash outside
made me rush to the window.
A phoenix! I thought.
But nothing was there
but one wriggling wish
waiting to be noticed
and a pretty thrush
wiping its nose on a fence post.

Yes

You must say *Yes*, said the Commissioner
and the Gauleiter and the Priest and
their wet-lipped toadies.

They said it to the writer burying his poems,
to the woman going mad in a pink suburb,
they said it to the firing squad.

They said it to technology,
to philosophy, to stubborn science.

They even said it to the child
walking hand in hand with his mother.

And God trembled
like a man caught
with the imprint of the gun butt
still on his palm.

How to cover the ground

One autumn, a jobbing gardener and I
dug over a lady's suburban garden.
When we finished, he looked at the dark clods
and said, with satisfaction,
That's the way I like to see it—
none o' they bloody floo'ers.

A fundamentalist. His view, not mine;
for I still ignorantly cherish
my flibbertigibbet fripperies
that elaborately hide
the ground I came from
and, in due season, will return to.

Rewards and furies

In a ship hardly bigger than this room,
with a mind narrower than this pen,
with a library of one book
and that book with one word in it,
Columbus sailed and sailed and arrived.

The poor soul didn't know where.

Still, he succeeded:
Indians were massacred, railways
opened up wheatfields, jails and asylums,
and skyscrapers walked around
with atom bombs slung at their hips.

I hope Columbus didn't believe
in his own ghost. How could it rest
through these hundreds of years?
How could it stare into the future
at his monstrous descendants
ignorantly sailing, ignorantly arriving?

Before posting

What will this hold,
this envelope on the table beside me?

I look out at the autumn day.
Brown leaves on blue sky.
And a host of pigeons, homely angels,
praising the Lord between heaven and earth.

The brown envelope will enclose them all,
and the microbes of loss,
the filthy paws of distance
and the gentle candles of love.

I cram myself into it
and, sitting here,
write on it your name.

Seen in the city

In the garden you walk the way
a tall flower would walk
in the music of Debussy.

The trees are fat now and heavy with blossom.
How slender you are
in their beautiful, podgy circle.

You call to your dog
who's bursting through the undergrowth
like a small black tank
on a tropical island.
He's filling himself with smells.

(A butterfly, crazy with wings,
is trying to go in every direction
at once.)

You stand still and the little dog
trundles flat out across the grass
to your feet. He sits down, panting,
and puts to shame the brightest flower in the garden
with two inches of tongue.

Bruce and that spider

The spider tried again.
It was too stupid to learn from experience.

It swung like a black watch on a silver thread
before Bruce's face.

As swung watches do, it began
to hypnotise him.

Bruce shook his Norman head and muttered,
Damn the brute, I'm getting out of here.

And, being too stupid to learn from experience,
he fought the Battle of Bannockburn. And won.

Moral? Experience teaches
that it doesn't.

A sort of physics

A tattery rosebush at a road corner
makes jubilant
a surly morning.
— And the song you begin to sing is cut short
by the dulled eye of a dead bird.

Archimedes was right. Give him a lever long enough
and he'd lift the world.

Even a moment, that weak and childish thing
that never grows out of childhood,
can tilt the world squint
with a lever as long as a wild rose petal,
as powerful
as the eye of a dead bird.

Archimedes was right, because his truths
contained others. He looked out from his one
into the weights and measures
of passion and hate and grief
where men spend lifetimes making
botched circles and trying to lift
immovable ounces.

(Though sometimes Rembrandt appears, or
Sophocles, or Mozart, and the uplifted world
sings a new song, a sad one and a merry one,
in the charnel house of space.)

Pastoral

The road folds itself half round a tree
and sets off at a new angle, seeming
pleased with the change.

It's not much of a road. It's been made
more by carts than men.

It bumps its nose against Lachie's house
and stops there
in the blue scent a peat fire makes,
in the cosy noises the brown hens make.

The cock, in the amazing uniform
of a wildly foreign Field Marshal,
scans two worlds through his monoculars.

— No enemy in sight. . .The Field Marshal becomes
a Pioneer Corps private in drag
and half-heartedly scratches the scratches
on the homely ground.

Recipe

You have to be stubborn.
You have to turn away
from meditation, from ideologies,
from the tombstone face
of the Royal Bank of Scotland.

You have to keep stubbornly saying
This is bread, though it's in a sunset,
this is a sunset with bread in it.
This is a woman, she doesn't live
in a book or an imagination.
Hello, water, you must say, Hello, good water.

You have to touch wood, but not for luck.
You have to listen to that matter of pitches and crescendos
without thinking Beethoven is speaking
only to you.

And you must learn there are words
with no meaning, words like *consolation*,
words like *goodbye*.

Go away, Ariel

Heartless, musical Ariel,
does everyone prefer Caliban to you,
as I do?

Supersonic Ariel, go zip round the world
or curl up in a cowslip's bell.
I'd rather be visited by Caliban.

As I am, I am. I chat with him
helplessly spilling out of an armchair,
scaly on the carpet.

I'm teaching him to smoke. It soothes him
when he blubbers about Miranda and
goes on about his mother.

Phone a bat, Ariel. Leave us
to have a good cry — to stare at each other
with recognition and loathing.

In that other world

They sit at their long table
in a room so long it's a tunnel,
in a tunnel with a green roof
on which sometimes a flower nods
as if to remind them of something.

They talk about everything
except Death, but they don't listen
to each other. They talk, staring
straight in front of them.
And they tremble.

The only time they notice each other
is when Death sweeps past them
with his keys clinking and a long pen
in his hand.

Then they look shyly at each other
for a moment before staring ahead
and talking, talking, trying to remember
what a flower is,
trying to remember
why they are here.

Foggy night

We put the tea things on the table
and turn on the TV for the News.
I look at the brown teapot, almost expecting it
to cluck.

Night is heavy on the city.
The lights struggle and on the Firth of Forth
a foghorn is suffering.

But space, good space, does not desert us.
In it the clock's voice plods on the mantelpiece
and a petal falls on the table.

The line of its fall is a fence
between the millions of years that have gone
and the millions to come.

Theologian

He tried to balance
the theory of predestination
on top of the theory of free will.
It kept tumbling down.

So he tried to balance
the theory of free will
on top of the theory of predestination.

He spent all day doing this.
But neither would stay on top.

In the evening he played another game.
He made a model of Justice
with her famous scales
and delicately put predestination
in one pan
and free will in the other.

They balanced.

He was disgusted. He growled
There's no justice in the world.

How could he know that Justice
was winking at him
behind her blindfold?

Old man

I am told (by me) to leave the fire
and go out into the wind and rain
like a starving hunter to bring back food
to the cave of my mind.

But my bow is broken, my arrows
without flight-feathers.

I feed on memories, a thin diet.
their waves tumble over each other,
their creatures move learnedly
in a sad nowhere at all.

Death is a playboy, and a cruel one.

. . .I look at the fire, at the dresser,
at the garish calendar.
I savour them. . . Keep the door shut.
There's food here in plenty.
It'll last till the coming of the playboy king,
capering and giggling yet again
at his one bad joke.

Walking alone

The moon makes this one the sort of night
where everything's delicate except the blunt shadows.

I'm unaware of walking — Pollóchan's house
meets me and passes me.

Thoughts come to me, but only from outside . . .
You're far away. And the distance is sighing.

Everything so wavers towards nothingness
I think I can't think of you.

— Here's the gate. It stands
in a blunt shadow.

There's a cushion of moss on the wall top
and out of it grows one trembling grass.

I go in: and sleep. And my sleep is
a cushion of moss where a dream trembles.

To a dead friend

I don't wish I could meet you again
on the other side of the broad river
that's as narrow
as the thinnest of threads.

If I did (and you could know it)
you'd be troubled, you'd blame yourself,
murmuring, *Have I, by only dying,*
blurred his mind into accepting
a comforting fantasy?

So I'm not impatient with the world
though you're not in it. I love it as I did
(when you were in it)
as I travel daily and helplessly
to that thinnest of threads,
that black river,
that destroyer of memory.

Trapped

Man, frantic with admiration
for the gray mess inside his skull,
invented the wheel, which turned into
a bicycle and a fighter plane.

He invented hygiene, which turned into
interesting new diseases.

He invented an afterlife and can't wait
to go into it.

He hasn't yet invented
a way of inventing
his afterself.

If only he were more like the stars,
conventionally exploding into life
and out of it, with no arguments
about abortion and euthanasia.

— Look, a new thought has appeared
in the brain of Professor Cedilla.
He doesn't know it, but it's shaped
like a boomerang and it knows
where it's going.

John Brown and Queen Victoria

He smooths his kilt, strokes
his Dundreary whiskers
and stares gloomily
at the hills behind Balmoral.
It's a tricky business
shuttling between
Your Majesty and *Vicky*.

The hills behind Balmoral
stare gloomily back at him.
They're practising purple
for the Queen's watercolours.

There are mobs there, of things like
grouse and deer. She
and her ghastly friends
will deal with them.

How familiar dare he be today?
Is she going to be *Your Majesty* or *Vicky?*

It's a tricky business, he thinks,
and smooths his kilt
that's two inches too long.

Buckingham Palace! — he wishes
he were there, away from
clarsachs and midgy picnics
and these damn sniggering gillies.

Disagreement

A little darkness is a good thing
to put on a bad thing, he said
— on a hurt brain or a bomb burst
or a dead sweetheart —
even on a sob, he said.
Tear a piece of darkness off the big darkness.
It makes a fine bandage.

I thought not.
I'd rather drain a drop of brightness
from the big brightness
and drink it down, so that I could look
right through the little darkness
to the big one and see there, with new clarity,
my people, my friends, my enemies
and the whole sick world
reeling through nightmares with lips tight shut
and closed eyes.

In folds of fire

In folds of fire — there's a fine-sounding phrase.
The reality
is different. . .

Creatures bolt in panic
in front of the roaring tidal wave
of a blazing forest.

Or love burns its candle and into it
jump the biggest of men
and the tallest of women.

Like Shadrach, Meshach and Abednego
they stroll
in the sexual flame.

In folds of fire. — What a mean
and narrow sound for what encloses
a candle flame and a fiery forest.

Dreams

The farmers are walking about
in their soggy fields. Inside their heads
a pleasant sun shines on crops without weeds.

In a house across the road a young man
plays a piano, aware of Bach and Bartók
listening indulgently to his blundering counterpoint.

And the dog asleep in a doorway twitches
his forepaws. He's chasing
the fattest hare in Midlothian.

Dreams fly everywhere. They creep
into minds whose owners have slammed them shut.
That boy's lungs are full of them.

Sometimes they come true and the world stares
at a new great painting or a body by the wayside
with chopped off hands.

The dreams of sleep dissolve when the window whitens
and the dreams of daylight swarm in with a passport to heaven
in one hand and a passport to hell in the other.

And sweet berries grow over the graves
of all of us or a white stone marks the place
which is the end of dreams, and of hell, and of heaven.

A matter of scale

My troubles and griefs
may seem ordinary to you, my friend,
but they make me a Lilliputian
in a world of Gullivers.

I try to avoid
their huge feet. When one of them
picks me up
I hold on to him
so as not to be blown away
by the wild stink of his breath.

While somewhere something
tosses the world in its hand,
judging its weight,
wondering if it's worth keeping.

Down and out

In a quarter of the city
where the streets try not to be noticed
Hope — in her old-fashioned clothes,
with her neglected hair-do —
pushes a pram.

Children try to play
but don't know how to.
Men with slack faces
lean on walls.

Hope trudges on, unnoticed
by everyone — except one old woman
who coos and gurgles over the pram
and the doll in it staring
at the nothing in nowhere
with manic blue eyes.

The first of them

The snake weeps below the tree.
He has been hated for so long.

Even Adam and Eve
were no sooner past that fiery sword
than they began to abuse him.

And the things that have been said about him
ever since — by parents to children,
by priests and lawmakers.

Poor snake. He crawls on his belly
dropping amber tears in the dust and whining
I was only obeying orders.

Queen of Scots

Mary was depressed.
She hadn't combed her red hair yet.
She hadn't touched her frightful Scottish breakfast.
Her lady-in-waiting, another Mary,
had told Rizzio Her Majesty wasn't at home,
a lie so obvious it was another way
of telling the truth.

Mary was depressed.
She wanted real life and here she was
acting in a real play, with real blood in it.

And she thought of the years to come
and of the frightful plays that would be written
about the play she was in.

She said something in French
and with her royal foot she kicked
the spaniel that was gazing at her
with exophthalmic adoration.

Bullfinch on guard in a hawthorn tree

Halberdier bullfinch
sticks out his chest
in a royal court of mayflowers.

Too still for spies. Too quiet for assassinations.

How imagine the mazy corridors unravelled
by ambassadors and cardinals?

The gentle sun cobwebs brightly
his black cap, his crimson breastplate.

Can a dream dream? Is there a Beauty sleeping
in a tiny chamber of leaves and small twigs?

He sees me and — duty calls — utters
his feeble, creaking, trisyllabic, piping call.

In Hades

The shades drank from the ditch of blood
and talked with Aeneas.
He was not only pious, he was clever
and knew how to change their bat-squeaks
to brave baritones.

One of them said nothing. He stood
at the fringe of the crowd, looking sadder and sadder.

When Aeneas went off to found an empire —
he was not only pious, he was stupid —
they rounded on him —
Where are your manners?
Is there no friendliness in Hell?

And he moved away into the darkest
of the dark shadows. He'd had enough
of blood, he'd had enough of empires.
He was content to be in the one place
whose hospitality was unlimited
and would last forever.

Neanderthal man

If we met, I reckon I'd be
the one to be frightened,
seeing in you
what civilisation has failed to destroy
in me.

I'd rush back to my libraries,
my knives and forks,
my barbers and musicians,
leaving you twirling your club
and stupidly looking for
the spoor of the future
you think has escaped you.